1. SUMMER SKY RIPPLE

Finished Size: Approximately 46" x 63"

MATERIALS

Worsted Weight Yarn, approximately:
- Color A (Blue) - 22 ounces, (620 grams, 1,445 yards)
- Color B (Yellow) - 10 ounces, (280 grams, 655 yards)
- Color C (Dark Blue) - 9 ounces, (260 grams, 590 yards)

Crochet hook, size H (5.00 mm) **or** size needed for gauge

GAUGE: One repeat from point to point = 3½"
and 6 rows = 4"

Gauge Swatch: (7" x 4")
Ch 35 **loosely**.
Work same as Afghan for 6 rows.
Finish off.

PATTERN STITCHES

BEGINNING CLUSTER (uses first 3 sts)
Ch 2, turn; ★ YO, insert hook in **next** st, YO and pull up a loop, YO and draw through 2 loops on hook; repeat from ★ once **more**, YO and draw through all 3 loops on hook.

CLUSTER (uses next 5 sts)
YO, insert hook in **next** st, YO and pull up a loop, YO and draw through 2 loops on hook, ★ YO, skip **next** ch, insert hook in **next** st, YO and pull up a loop, YO and draw through 2 loops on hook; repeat from ★ once **more**, YO and draw through all 4 loops on hook.

ENDING CLUSTER (uses last 3 sts)
★ YO, insert hook in **next** st, YO and pull up a loop, YO and draw through 2 loops on hook; repeat from ★ 2 times **more**, YO and draw through all 4 loops on hook.

COLOR SEQ
2 Rows **each**: C
Color A, Color B
(Fig. 3, page 1)

With Color A, ch 211 **loosely**.

Row 1 (Right side)**:** YO, insert hook in fourth ch from hook, YO and pull up a loop, YO and draw through 2 loops on hook, YO, insert hook in next ch, YO and pull up a loop, YO and draw through 2 loops on hook, YO and draw through all 3 loops on hook, ch 1, skip next 2 chs, 5 dc in next ch, ch 1, skip next 2 chs, 7 dc in next ch, ch 1, skip next 2 chs, 5 dc in next ch, ch 1, ★ skip next 2 chs, work Cluster, ch 1, skip next 2 chs, 5 dc in next ch, ch 1, skip next 2 chs, 7 dc in next ch, ch 1, skip next 2 chs, 5 dc in next ch, ch 1; repeat from ★ across to last 5 chs, skip next 2 chs, work ending Cluster: 235 sts and 52 ch-1 sps.

Row 2: Working in Back Loops Only ***(Fig. 1, page 1)***, work beginning Cluster, ch 1, skip next 4 dc, 5 dc in next ch, ch 1, skip next 3 dc, 7 dc in next dc, ch 1, skip next 3 dc, 5 dc in next ch, ch 1, ★ skip next 4 dc, work Cluster, ch 1, skip next 4 dc, 5 dc in next ch, ch 1, skip next 3 dc, 7 dc in next dc, ch 1, skip next 3 dc, 5 dc in next ch, ch 1; repeat from ★ across to last 7 sts, skip next 4 dc, work ending Cluster.

Repeat Row 2 until Afghan measures approximately 63" from beginning ch, ending by working 2 rows Color A.

Finish off.

CROCHET TERMINOLOGY	
UNITED STATES	**INTERNATIONAL**
slip stitch (slip st)	= single crochet (sc)
single crochet (sc)	= double crochet (dc)
half double crochet (hdc)	= half treble crochet (htr)
double crochet (dc)	= treble crochet (tr)
treble crochet (tr)	= double treble crochet (dtr)
double treble crochet (dtr)	= triple treble crochet (ttr)
skip	= miss

ALUMINUM CROCHET HOOKS													
U.S.	B-1	C-2	D-3	E-4	F-5	G-6	H-8	I-9	J-10	K-10½	N	P	Q
Metric - mm	2.25	2.75	3.25	3.50	3.75	4.00	5.00	5.50	6.00	6.50	9.00	10.00	15.00

8

11

2. CABLES & CONTOURS RIPPLE

Finished Size: Approximately 49" x 63"

MATERIALS

Worsted Weight Yarn, approximately:
Color A (Dark Pink) - 13 ounces, (370 grams, 965 yards)
Color B (Pink) - 11 ounces, (310 grams, 815 yards)
Color C (Light Pink) - 12 ounces, (340 grams, 890 yards)
Crochet hook, size H (5.00 mm) **or** size needed for gauge

GAUGE: One repeat from point to point = 7¼" and 6 rows = 4¼"

Gauge Swatch: (12¼" x 4¼")
Ch 54 **loosely**.
Work same as Afghan for 6 rows.
Finish off.

PATTERN STITCHES

CLUSTER (uses next 3 sts)
★ YO, insert hook in **next** st, YO and pull up a loop, YO and draw through 2 loops on hook; repeat from ★ 2 times **more**, YO and draw through all 4 loops on hook.

TREBLE CROCHET ***(abbreviated tr)***
YO twice, insert hook in st indicated, YO and pull up a loop, (YO and draw through 2 loops on hook) 3 times.

BACK POST TREBLE CROCHET ***(abbreviated BPtr)***
YO twice, insert hook from **back** to **front** around post of st indicated ***(Fig. 4, page 1)***, YO and pull up a loop, (YO and draw through 2 loops on hook) 3 times. Skip st in front of BPtr.

FRONT POST DOUBLE TREBLE CROCHET ***(abbreviated FPdtr)***
YO 3 times, insert hook from **front** to **back** around post of st indicated ***(Fig. 4, page 1)***, YO and pull up a loop, (YO and draw through 2 loops on hook) 4 times. Skip st behind FPdtr.

CABLE
Skip next 2 BPtr, work FPdtr around each of next 2 BPtr ***(Fig. 6a)***, working in **front** of 2 FPdtr just made, work FPdtr around first skipped BPtr and around next skipped BPtr ***(Fig. 6b)***.

Fig. 6a

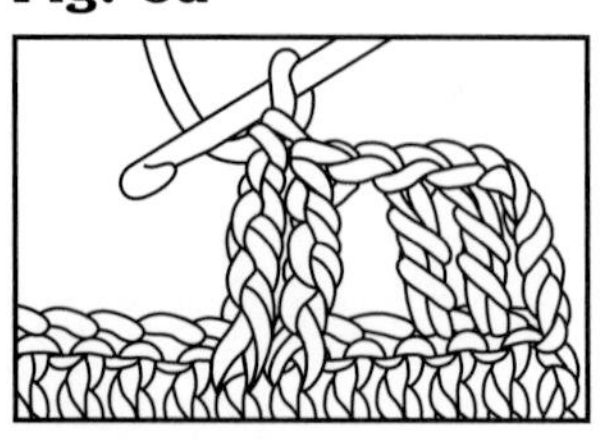

Fig. 6b

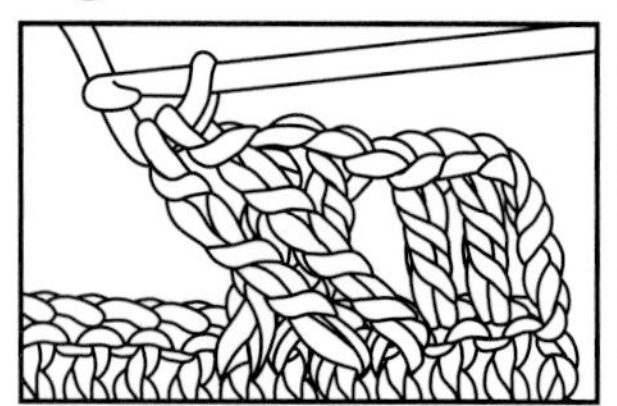

COLOR SEQUENCE
4 Rows **each**: Color A, ★ Color B, Color C, Color A; repeat from ★ throughout ***(Fig. 3, page 1)***.

With Color A, ch 199 **loosely**.

Row 1 (Right side)**:** YO, insert hook in fourth ch from hook **(3 skipped chs count as first dc)**, YO and pull up a loop, YO and draw through 2 loops on hook, (YO, insert hook in **next** ch, YO and pull up a loop, YO and draw through 2 loops on hook) twice, YO and draw through all 4 loops on hook, dc in next 7 chs, 5 dc in next ch, dc in next 7 chs, work Cluster, dc in next ch, ★ ch 1, skip next ch, tr in next ch, skip next ch, 2 tr in next ch, working around 2 tr just made, 2 tr in skipped ch, tr in next ch, ch 1, skip next ch, dc in next ch, work Cluster, dc in next 7 chs, 5 dc in next ch, dc in next 7 chs, work Cluster, dc in next ch; repeat from ★ across: 197 sts and 12 ch-1 sps.

Row 2: Ch 3 **(counts as first dc, now and throughout)**, turn; work Cluster, dc in next 7 dc, 5 dc in next dc, dc in next 7 dc, work Cluster, dc in next dc, ★ ch 1, tr in next tr, work BPtr around each of next 4 tr, tr in next tr, ch 1, dc in next dc, work Cluster, dc in next 7 dc, 5 dc in next dc, dc in next 7 dc, work Cluster, dc in next dc; repeat from ★ across.

Row 3: Ch 3, turn; work Cluster, dc in next 7 dc, 5 dc in next dc, dc in next 7 dc, work Cluster, dc in next dc, ★ ch 1, tr in next tr, work Cable ***(Figs. 6a & b)***, tr in next tr, ch 1, dc in next dc, work Cluster, dc in next 7 dc, 5 dc in next dc, dc in next 7 dc, work Cluster, dc in next dc; repeat from ★ across.

Row 4: Ch 3, turn; work Cluster, dc in next 7 dc, 5 dc in next dc, dc in next 7 dc, work Cluster, dc in next dc, ★ ch 1, tr in next tr, work BPtr around each of next 4 FPdtr, tr in next tr, ch 1, dc in next dc, work Cluster, dc in next 7 dc, 5 dc in next dc, dc in next 7 dc, work Cluster, dc in next dc; repeat from ★ across.

Repeat Rows 3 and 4 until Afghan measures approximately 63" from beginning ch, ending by working 4 rows Color A.

Finish off.

3. ANTIQUE TEAL RIPPLE

Finished Size: Approximately 46" x 61"

MATERIALS

Worsted Weight Yarn, approximately:
- Color A (Dark Teal) - 9 ounces, (260 grams, 670 yards)
- Color B (Light Teal) - 17 ounces, (480 grams, 1,265 yards)
- Color C (Teal) - 9 ounces, (260 grams, 670 yards)

Crochet hook, size I (5.50 mm) **or** size needed for gauge

GAUGE: One repeat from point to point = 3½"
and 6 rows = 4"

Gauge Swatch: (7" x 4")
Ch 41 **loosely**.
Work same as Afghan for 6 rows.
Finish off.

PATTERN STITCHES

SHELL

(2 Dc, ch 3, 2 dc) in st or sp indicated.

LONG DOUBLE CROCHET *(abbreviated LDC)*

YO, working around next ch-2, insert hook in st or sp indicated one row **below**, YO and pull up a loop even with last st made, (YO and draw through 2 loops on hook) twice.

COLOR SEQUENCE

2 Rows **each**: Color A, ★ Color B, Color C, Color B, Color A; repeat from ★ throughout ***(Fig. 3, page 1)***.

With Color A, ch 261 **loosely**.

Row 1 (Right side)**:** Dc in fourth ch from hook **(3 skipped chs count as first dc)**, ch 2, skip next 3 chs, 2 dc in next ch, ch 2, skip next 3 chs, work Shell in next ch, ★ (ch 2, skip next 3 chs, 2 dc in next ch) twice, (skip next 3 chs, 2 dc in next ch, ch 2) twice, skip next 3 chs, work Shell in next ch; repeat from ★ 11 times **more**, ch 2, skip next 3 chs, 2 dc in next ch, ch 2, skip next 3 chs, dc in last 2 chs: 156 dc and 65 sps.

Row 2: Ch 3 **(counts as first dc, now and throughout)**, turn; skip next dc, work LDC in center ch of first 3 skipped chs on beginning ch, ch 2, skip next 2 dc, work 2 LDC in center ch of next 3 skipped chs on beginning ch, ch 2, skip next 2 dc, work Shell in next ch-3 sp, ★ (ch 2, skip next 2 dc, work 2 LDC in center ch of next 3 skipped chs on beginning ch) twice, skip next 4 dc, (work 2 LDC in center ch of next 3 skipped chs on beginning ch, ch 2, skip next 2 dc) twice, work Shell in next ch-3 sp; repeat from ★ 11 times **more**, ch 2, skip next 2 dc, work 2 LDC in center ch of next 3 skipped chs on beginning ch, ch 2, skip next 2 dc, work LDC in center ch of last 3 skipped chs on beginning ch, skip next dc, dc in last dc.

Row 3: Ch 3, turn; skip next LDC, work 2 LDC in sp **between** next 2 dc (one row **below**), ch 2, skip next 2 LDC, work 2 LDC in sp **between** next 2 dc, ch 2, skip next 2 dc, work Shell in next ch-3 sp, ch 2, skip next 2 dc, work 2 LDC in sp **between** next 2 dc, ch 2, skip next 2 LDC, work 2 LDC in sp **between** next 2 dc, ★ skip next 4 LDC, work 2 LDC in sp **between** next 2 dc, ch 2, skip next 2 LDC, work 2 LDC in sp **between** next 2 dc, ch 2, skip next 2 dc, work Shell in next ch-3 sp, ch 2, skip next 2 dc, work 2 LDC in sp **between** next 2 dc, ch 2, skip next 2 LDC, work 2 LDC in sp **between** next 2 dc; repeat from ★ 11 times **more**, skip next LDC, dc in last dc.

Row 4: Ch 3, turn; skip next 2 LDC, work 2 LDC in sp **between** next 2 LDC (one row **below**), ch 2, skip next 2 LDC, work 2 LDC in sp **between** next 2 dc, ch 2, skip next 2 dc, work Shell in next ch-3 sp, ch 2, skip next 2 dc, work 2 LDC in sp **between** next 2 dc, ch 2, skip next 2 LDC, work 2 LDC in sp **between** next 2 LDC, ★ skip next 4 LDC, work 2 LDC in sp **between** next 2 LDC, ch 2, skip next 2 LDC, work 2 LDC in sp **between** next 2 dc, ch 2, skip next 2 dc, work Shell in next ch-3 sp, ch 2, skip next 2 dc, work 2 LDC in sp **between** next 2 dc, ch 2, skip next 2 LDC, work 2 LDC in sp **between** next 2 LDC; repeat from ★ 11 times **more**, skip next 2 LDC, dc in last dc.

Repeat Row 4 until Afghan measures approximately 60" from beginning ch, ending by working one row Color A; do **not** finish off.

Last Row: Ch 3, turn; skip next 2 LDC, work 2 LDC in sp **between** next 2 LDC (one row **below**), sc in next 2 LDC, work 2 LDC in sp **between** next 2 dc, sc in next 2 dc, (sc, ch 3, sc) in next ch-3 sp, sc in next 2 dc, work 2 LDC in sp **between** next 2 dc, sc in next 2 LDC, work 2 LDC in sp **between** next 2 LDC, ★ skip next 4 LDC, work 2 LDC in sp **between** next 2 LDC, sc in next 2 LDC, work 2 LDC in sp **between** next 2 dc, sc in next 2 dc, (sc, ch 3, sc) in next ch-3 sp, sc in next 2 dc, work 2 LDC in sp **between** next 2 dc, sc in next 2 LDC, work 2 LDC in sp **between** next 2 LDC; repeat from ★ 11 times **more**, skip next 2 LDC, dc in last dc; finish off.

15

3
A PRESENT
for

4. WATERFALL RIPPLE

Finished Size: Approximately 44" x 62"

MATERIALS

Worsted Weight Yarn, approximately:
- Color A (Dark Blue) - 6 ounces, (170 grams, 395 yards)
- Color B (Medium Blue) - 9 ounces, (260 grams, 590 yards)
- Color C (Blue) - 10 ounces, (280 grams, 655 yards)
- Color D (Light Blue) - 10 ounces, (280 grams, 655 yards)
- Color E (White) - 5 ounces, (140 grams, 330 yards)

Crochet hook, size H (5.00 mm) **or** size needed for gauge

GAUGE: One repeat from point to point = $5\frac{1}{2}$"
and 6 rows = $4\frac{1}{2}$"

Gauge Swatch: (11" x $4\frac{1}{2}$")
Ch 50 **loosely**.
Work same as Afghan for 6 rows.
Finish off.

PATTERN STITCHES

BEGINNING CLUSTER (uses first 3 sts)
Ch 2, turn; ★ YO, insert hook in **next** st, YO and pull up a loop, YO and draw through 2 loops on hook; repeat from ★ once **more**, YO and draw through all 3 loops on hook.

CLUSTER (uses next 5 sts)
★ YO, insert hook in **next** st, YO and pull up a loop, YO and draw through 2 loops on hook; repeat from ★ 4 times **more**, YO and draw through all 6 loops on hook.

ENDING CLUSTER (uses last 3 sts)
★ YO, insert hook in **next** st, YO and pull up a loop, YO and draw through 2 loops on hook; repeat from ★ 2 times **more**, YO and draw through all 4 loops on hook.

LONG FRONT POST TREBLE CROCHET ***(abbreviated LFPtr)***
YO twice, insert hook from **front** to **back** around post of dc 2 rows **below** next dc ***(Fig. 7a)***, YO and pull up a loop even with last st made ***(Fig. 7b)***, (YO and draw through 2 loops on hook) 3 times. Skip dc behind LFPtr.

Fig. 7a

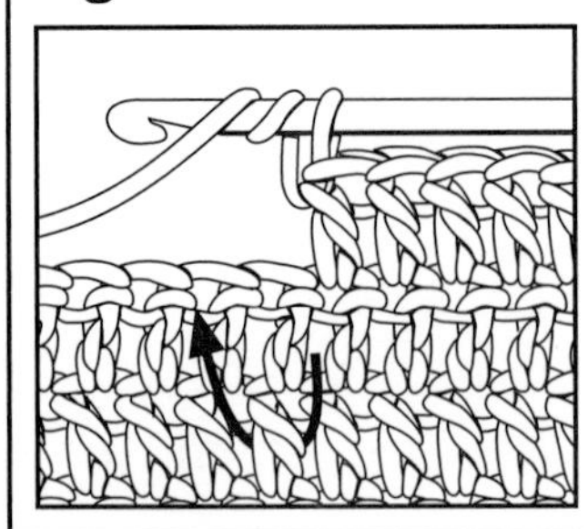

Fig. 7b

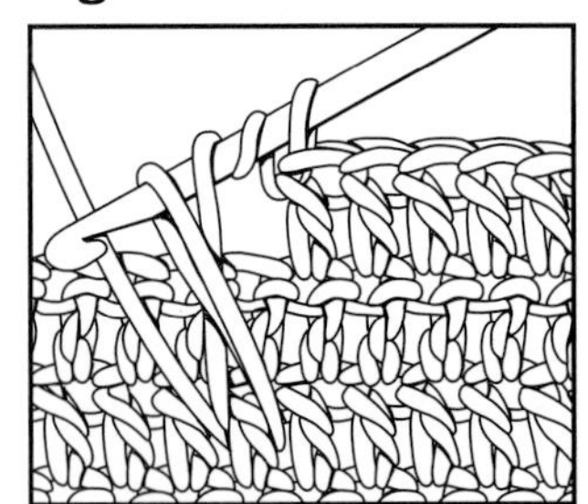

COLOR SEQUENCE

2 Rows **each**: Color A, ★ Color B, Color C, Color D, Color E, Color D, Color C, Color B, Color A; repeat from ★ throughout ***(Fig. 3, page 1)***.

With Color A, ch 194 **loosely**.

Row 1 (Right side)**:** YO, insert hook in third ch from hook, YO and pull up a loop, YO and draw through 2 loops on hook, YO, insert hook in next ch, YO and pull up a loop, YO and draw through 2 loops on hook, YO and draw through all 3 loops on hook, dc in next 9 chs, 5 dc in next ch, dc in next 9 chs, ★ work Cluster, dc in next 9 chs, 5 dc in next ch, dc in next 9 chs; repeat from ★ across to last 3 chs, work ending Cluster: 193 sts.

Row 2: Work beginning Cluster, dc in next 9 dc, 5 dc in next dc, dc in next 9 dc, ★ work Cluster, dc in next 9 dc, 5 dc in next dc, dc in next 9 dc; repeat from ★ across to last 3 sts, work ending Cluster.

Row 3: Work beginning Cluster, dc in next 5 dc, work LFPtr ***(Figs. 7a & b)***, dc in next 3 dc, 5 dc in next dc, dc in next 3 dc, work LFPtr, dc in next 5 dc, ★ work Cluster, dc in next 5 dc, work LFPtr, dc in next 3 dc, 5 dc in next dc, dc in next 3 dc, work LFPtr, dc in next 5 dc; repeat from ★ across to last 3 sts, work ending Cluster.

Row 4: Work beginning Cluster, dc in next 9 sts, 5 dc in next dc, dc in next 9 sts, ★ work Cluster, dc in next 9 sts, 5 dc in next dc, dc in next 9 sts; repeat from ★ across to last 3 sts, work ending Cluster.

Repeat Rows 3 and 4 until Afghan measures approximately 62" from beginning ch, ending by working 2 rows Color A.

Finish off.

5. PEACHES & CREAM RIPPLE

Finished Size: Approximately 45" x 62"

MATERIALS

Worsted Weight Yarn, approximately:
Color A (Dark Peach) - 15 ounces, (430 grams, 985 yards)
Color B (Peach) - 12 ounces, (340 grams, 790 yards)
Color C (Ecru) - 17 ounces, (480 grams, 1,115 yards)
Crochet hook, size H (5.00 mm) **or** size needed for gauge

GAUGE: One repeat from point to point = $4^{1}/_{2}$"
and 6 rows = 4"

Gauge Swatch: (9" x 4")
Ch 39 **loosely**.
Work same as Afghan for 6 rows.
Finish off.

PATTERN STITCHES

CLUSTER (uses next 3 sts)
★ YO, insert hook in **next** st, YO and pull up a loop, YO and draw through 2 loops on hook; repeat from ★ 2 times **more**, YO and draw through all 4 loops on hook.

POPCORN
4 Dc in dc indicated, drop loop from hook, insert hook in first dc of 4-dc group, hook dropped loop and draw through.

COLOR SEQUENCE
2 Rows **each**: Color A, ★ Color B, Color C, Color A; repeat from ★ throughout ***(Fig. 3, page 1)***.

With Color A, ch 183 **loosely**.

Row 1 (Right side)**:** 2 Dc in fourth ch from hook **(3 skipped chs count as first dc)**, dc in next 5 chs, work 2 Clusters, dc in next 5 chs, ★ 3 dc in each of next 2 chs, dc in next 5 chs, work 2 Clusters, dc in next 5 chs; repeat from ★ across to last ch, 3 dc in last ch: 180 sts.

Note: Loop a short piece of yarn around any stitch to mark last row as **right** side.

Row 2: Ch 3 **(counts as first dc, now and throughout)**, turn; 2 dc in same st, dc in next 5 dc, work 2 Clusters, dc in next 5 dc, ★ 3 dc in each of next 2 dc, dc in next 5 dc, work 2 Clusters, dc in next 5 dc; repeat from ★ across to last dc, 3 dc in last dc.

Rows 3 and 4: Ch 3, turn; 2 dc in same st, dc in next 5 dc, work 2 Clusters, dc in next 5 dc, ★ 3 dc in each of next 2 dc, dc in next 5 dc, work 2 Clusters, dc in next 5 dc; repeat from ★ across to last dc, 3 dc in last dc.

Row 5: Ch 3, turn; 2 dc in same st, work Popcorn in next dc, (ch 1, skip next dc, work Popcorn in next dc) twice, work 2 Clusters, work Popcorn in next dc, (ch 1, skip next dc, work Popcorn in next dc) twice, ★ 3 dc in each of next 2 dc, work Popcorn in next dc, (ch 1, skip next dc, work Popcorn in next dc) twice, work 2 Clusters, work Popcorn in next dc, (ch 1, skip next dc, work Popcorn in next dc) twice; repeat from ★ across to last dc, 3 dc in last dc.

Row 6: Ch 3, turn; 2 dc in same st, dc in next 5 sts, work 2 Clusters, dc in next 5 sts, ★ 3 dc in each of next 2 dc, dc in next 5 sts, work 2 Clusters, dc in next 5 sts; repeat from ★ across to last dc, 3 dc in last dc.

Rows 7 and 8: Ch 3, turn; 2 dc in same st, dc in next 5 dc, work 2 Clusters, dc in next 5 dc, ★ 3 dc in each of next 2 dc, dc in next 5 dc, work 2 Clusters, dc in next 5 dc; repeat from ★ across to last dc, 3 dc in last dc.

Repeat Rows 3-8 until Afghan measures approximately 62" from beginning ch, ending by working 2 rows Color A.

Finish off.

With Color A, add 12 strands of fringe at each point across short edges of Afghan ***(Figs. 5a & b, page 1)***.

4

16

6. ROSE PETAL RIPPLE

Finished Size: Approximately 46" x 61"

MATERIALS

Worsted Weight Yarn, approximately:
- Color A (Dark Pink) - 9 ounces, (260 grams, 590 yards)
- Color B (Pink) - 17 ounces, (480 grams, 1,115 yards)
- Color C (Light Pink) - 7 ounces, (200 grams, 460 yards)

Crochet hook, size I (5.50 mm) **or** size needed for gauge

GAUGE: One repeat from point to point = 3 1/4" and 4 rows = 3"

Gauge Swatch: (6 1/2" x 3")
Ch 28 **loosely**.
Work same as Afghan for 4 rows.
Finish off.

PATTERN STITCHES

CLUSTER (uses next 5 sts or sps)
★ YO, insert hook in **next** st or sp, YO and pull up a loop, YO and draw through 2 loops on hook; repeat from ★ 4 times **more**, YO and draw through all 6 loops on hook.

ENDING CLUSTER (uses last 4 sts)
YO, insert hook in **next** dc, YO and pull up a loop, YO and draw through 2 loops on hook, YO, skip next ch **and** next dc, insert hook in **last** st, YO and pull up a loop, YO and draw through 2 loops on hook, YO and draw through all 3 loops on hook.

COLOR SEQUENCE
One row **each**: Color A, ★ Color B, Color C, Color B, Color A; repeat from ★ throughout ***(Fig. 3, page 1)***.

With Color A, ch 184 **loosely**.

Row 1 (Right side)**:** Dc in fourth ch from hook, ch 1, skip next ch, dc in next ch, ch 1, skip next ch, 3 dc in next ch, ch 3, 3 dc in next ch, ch 1, skip next ch, dc in next ch, ch 1, ★ skip next ch, work Cluster, ch 1, skip next ch, dc in next ch, ch 1, skip next ch, 3 dc in next ch, ch 3, 3 dc in next ch, ch 1, skip next ch, dc in next ch, ch 1; repeat from ★ across to last 4 chs, (YO, skip **next** ch, insert hook in **next** ch, YO and pull up a loop, YO and draw through 2 loops on hook) twice, YO and draw through all 3 loops on hook: 128 sts and 70 sps.

Row 2: Ch 3, turn; (skip next ch, dc in next dc, ch 1) twice, (3 dc, ch 3, 3 dc) in next ch-3 sp, ch 1, skip next 2 dc, dc in next dc, ch 1, ★ skip next ch, work Cluster, ch 1, skip next ch, dc in next dc, ch 1, (3 dc, ch 3, 3 dc) in next ch-3 sp, ch 1, skip next 2 dc, dc in next dc, ch 1; repeat from ★ across to last 5 sts, skip next ch, work ending Cluster.

Repeat Row 2 until Afghan measures approximately 61" from beginning ch, ending by working one row Color A.

Finish off.

7. COLONIAL RIPPLE

Finished Size: Approximately 48" x 61"

MATERIALS

Worsted Weight Yarn, approximately:
Color A (Dark Blue) - 3 ounces, (90 grams, 195 yards)
Color B (Blue) - 8 ounces, (230 grams, 525 yards)
Color C (Tan) - 10 ounces, (280 grams, 655 yards)
Color D (Ecru) - 8 ounces, (230 grams, 525 yards)
Color E (Red) - 6 ounces, (170 grams, 395 yards)
Crochet hook, size H (5.00 mm) **or** size needed for gauge

GAUGE: One repeat from point to point and 8 rows = 6"

Gauge Swatch: (12" x 6")
Ch 61 **loosely**.
Work same as Afghan for 8 rows.
Finish off.

PATTERN STITCHES

3-DC CLUSTER (uses next 3 sts)
★ YO, insert hook in **next** st, YO and pull up a loop, YO and draw through 2 loops on hook; repeat from ★ 2 times **more**, YO and draw through all 4 loops on hook.

5-DC CLUSTER (uses next 5 sts)
★ YO, insert hook in **next** st, YO and pull up a loop, YO and draw through 2 loops on hook; repeat from ★ 4 times **more**, YO and draw through all 6 loops on hook.

COLOR SEQUENCE

One row **each**: Color A, ★ Color B, Color C, Color D, Color E, Color D, Color C, Color B, Color A; repeat from ★ throughout ***(Fig. 3, page 1)***.

With Color A, ch 229 **loosely**.

Row 1 (Right side)**:** YO, insert hook in fourth ch from hook **(3 skipped chs count as first dc)**, YO and pull up a loop, YO and draw through 2 loops on hook, (YO, insert hook in **next** ch, YO and pull up a loop, YO and draw through 2 loops on hook) twice, YO and draw through all 4 loops on hook, dc in next 11 chs, 5 dc in next ch, dc in next 11 chs, ★ work 5-dc Cluster, dc in next 11 chs, 5 dc in next ch, dc in next 11 chs; repeat from ★ across to last 4 chs, work 3-dc Cluster, dc in last ch: 227 sts.

Row 2: Ch 3 **(counts as first dc, now and throughout)**, turn; working in both loops, work 3-dc Cluster, ch 1, (skip next dc, dc in next dc, ch 1) 5 times, skip next dc, 5 dc in next dc, ch 1, (skip next dc, dc in next dc, ch 1) 5 times, ★ skip next dc, work 5-dc Cluster, ch 1, (skip next dc, dc in next dc, ch 1) 5 times, skip next dc, 5 dc in next dc, ch 1, (skip next dc, dc in next dc, ch 1) 5 times; repeat from ★ across to last 5 sts, skip next dc, work 3-dc Cluster, dc in last dc: 131 sts and 96 ch-1 sps.

Row 3: Ch 3, turn; working in Back Loops Only ***(Fig. 1, page 1)***, work 3-dc Cluster, dc in next 11 sts, 5 dc in next dc, dc in next 11 sts, ★ work 5-dc Cluster, dc in next 11 sts, 5 dc in next dc, dc in next 11 sts; repeat from ★ across to last 4 sts, work 3-dc Cluster, dc in last dc: 227 sts.

Repeat Rows 2 and 3 until Afghan measures approximately 61" from beginning ch, ending by working one row Color A.

Finish off.

13

12

8. GRANDMA'S LACY RIPPLE

Finished Size: Approximately 46" x 61"

MATERIALS

Worsted Weight Yarn, approximately:
32 ounces, (910 grams, 2,105 yards)
Crochet hook, size I (5.50 mm) **or** size needed for gauge

GAUGE: One repeat from point to point = 4¾"
and 4 rows = 3"

Gauge Swatch: (8¼" x 4¾")
Ch 36 **loosely**.
Work same as Afghan for 6 rows.
Finish off.

PATTERN STITCHES

3-DC SHELL
Dc in st indicated, (ch 1, dc in same st) twice.

5-DC SHELL
Dc in st or sp indicated, (ch 1, dc in same st or sp) 4 times.

Ch 212 **loosely**.

Row 1 (Right side)**:** Dc in fourth ch from hook and in next 4 chs **(3 skipped chs count as first dc)**, work 3-dc Shell in next ch, dc in next 5 chs, ★ skip next 5 chs, work 5-dc Shell in next ch, skip next 5 chs, dc in next 5 chs, work 3-dc Shell in next ch, dc in next 5 chs; repeat from ★ across: 176 dc and 56 ch-1 sps.

Row 2: Ch 3 **(counts as first dc, now and throughout)**, turn; skip next dc, dc in next 4 dc and in next ch-1 sp, work 3-dc Shell in next dc, dc in next ch-1 sp and in next 4 dc, ★ ch 1, skip next 4 dc, sc in next ch-1 sp, ch 4, sc in next ch-1 sp, ch 1, skip next 4 dc, dc in next 4 dc and in next ch-1 sp, work 3-dc Shell in next dc, dc in next ch-1 sp and in next 4 dc; repeat from ★ across to last 3 dc, leave last 3 dc unworked: 149 sts and 47 sps.

Row 3: Ch 3, turn; skip next dc, dc in next 4 dc and in next ch-1 sp, work 3-dc Shell in next dc, dc in next ch-1 sp and in next 4 dc, ★ skip next 4 sts, work 5-dc Shell in next ch-4 sp, skip next 2 dc, dc in next 4 dc and in next ch-1 sp, work 3-dc Shell in next dc, dc in next ch-1 sp and in next 4 dc; repeat from ★ across to last 3 dc, leave last 3 dc unworked: 176 dc and 56 ch-1 sps.

Repeat Rows 2 and 3 until Afghan measures approximately 61" from beginning ch, ending by working Row 3.

Finish off.

9. HOLLY & IVY RIPPLE

Finished Size: Approximately 48" x 57"

MATERIALS

Worsted Weight Yarn, approximately:
Color A (Maroon) - 10 ounces, (280 grams, 630 yards)
Color B (Natural) - 28 ounces, (800 grams, 1,760 yards)
Color C (Green) - 8 ounces, (230 grams, 505 yards)
Crochet hook, size H (5.00 mm) **or** size needed for gauge

GAUGE: One repeat from point to point = 4"
and 8 rows = 5"

Gauge Swatch: (8½" x 5")
Ch 39 **loosely**.
Work same as Afghan for 8 rows.
Finish off.

COLOR SEQUENCE

2 Rows Color A, one row **each**: Color B, Color C, Color B, 2 rows Color A, ★ 7 rows Color B, 2 rows Color C, one row **each**: Color B, Color A, Color B, 2 rows Color C, 7 rows Color B, 2 rows Color A, one row **each**: Color B, Color C, Color B, 2 rows Color A; repeat from ★ 2 times **more** ***(Fig. 3, page 1)***.

With Color A, ch 199 **loosely**.

Row 1 (Right side)**:** 3 Dc in seventh ch from hook **(6 skipped chs count as first dc plus ch 3)**, ★ (skip next 2 chs, 3 dc in next ch) twice, skip next 3 chs, (3 dc in next ch, skip next 2 chs) twice, (3 dc, ch 3, 3 dc) in next ch; repeat from ★ across: 220 dc and 13 ch-3 sps.

Row 2: Ch 6 **(counts as first dc plus ch 3)**, turn; 3 dc in first ch-3 sp, ★ (skip next 3 dc, 3 dc in sp **before** next dc) twice, skip next 6 dc, (3 dc in sp **before** next dc, skip next 3 dc) twice, (3 dc, ch 3, 3 dc) in next ch-3 sp; repeat from ★ across to last dc, leave last dc unworked.

Repeat Row 2 until Afghan measures approximately 57" from beginning ch, ending by working 2 rows Color A.

Finish off.

10. GOLDEN HARVEST RIPPLE

Finished Size: Approximately 48" x 64"

MATERIALS

Worsted Weight Yarn, approximately:
- Color A (Brown) - 19 ounces, (540 grams, 1,250 yards)
- Color B (Gold) - 8 ounces, (230 grams, 525 yards)
- Color C (Light Gold) - 8 ounces, (230 grams, 525 yards)
- Color D (Ecru) - 6 ounces, (170 grams, 395 yards)

Crochet hook, size H (5.00 mm) **or** size needed for gauge

GAUGE: One repeat from point to point and 8 rows = 4"

Gauge Swatch: (8½" x 4")
Ch 41 **loosely**.
Work same as Afghan for 8 rows.
Finish off.

PATTERN STITCHES

V-STITCH *(abbreviated V-St)*
(Dc, ch 1, dc) in st indicated.

CLUSTER (uses next 5 sts)
YO, insert hook in **next** st, YO and pull up a loop, YO and draw through 2 loops on hook, ★ YO, skip **next** st, insert hook in **next** st, YO and pull up a loop, YO and draw through 2 loops on hook; repeat from ★ once **more**, YO and draw through all 4 loops on hook.

COLOR SEQUENCE

8 Rows Color A, ★ 3 rows Color B, one row Color A, 3 rows Color C, one row Color B, 3 rows Color D, one row Color C, 8 rows Color A; repeat from ★ throughout ***(Fig. 3, page 1)***.

With Color A, ch 221 **loosely**.

Row 1 (Right side)**:** Dc in fifth ch from hook **(4 skipped chs count as first dc plus ch 1)**, (skip next ch, work V-St in next ch) twice, skip next 2 chs, work Cluster, ★ skip next 2 chs, (work V-St in next ch, skip next ch) twice, dc in next ch, (ch 1, dc in same st) twice, (skip next ch, work V-St in next ch) twice, skip next 2 chs, work Cluster; repeat from ★ 10 times **more**, skip next 2 chs, work V-St in next ch, (skip next ch, work V-St in next ch) twice: 145 sts and 72 ch-1 sps.

Note: Loop a short piece of yarn around any stitch to mark last row as **right** side.

Row 2: Ch 1, turn; sc in each st and in each ch-1 sp across: 217 sc.

Row 3: Ch 4 **(counts as first dc plus ch 1)**, turn; dc in same st, (skip next sc, work V-St in next sc) twice, skip next 2 sc, work Cluster, ★ skip next 2 sc, (work V-St in next sc, skip next sc) twice, dc in next sc, (ch 1, dc in same st) twice, (skip next sc, work V-St in next sc) twice, skip next 2 sc, work Cluster; repeat from ★ 10 times **more**, skip next 2 sc, work V-St in next sc, (skip next sc, work V-St in next sc) twice.

Row 4: Ch 1, turn; sc in each st and in each ch-1 sp across.

Repeat Rows 3 and 4 until Afghan measures approximately 64" from beginning ch, ending by working 8 rows Color A.

Finish off.

With Color A, add 12 strands of fringe at each point across short edges of Afghan ***(Figs. 5a & b, page 1)***.

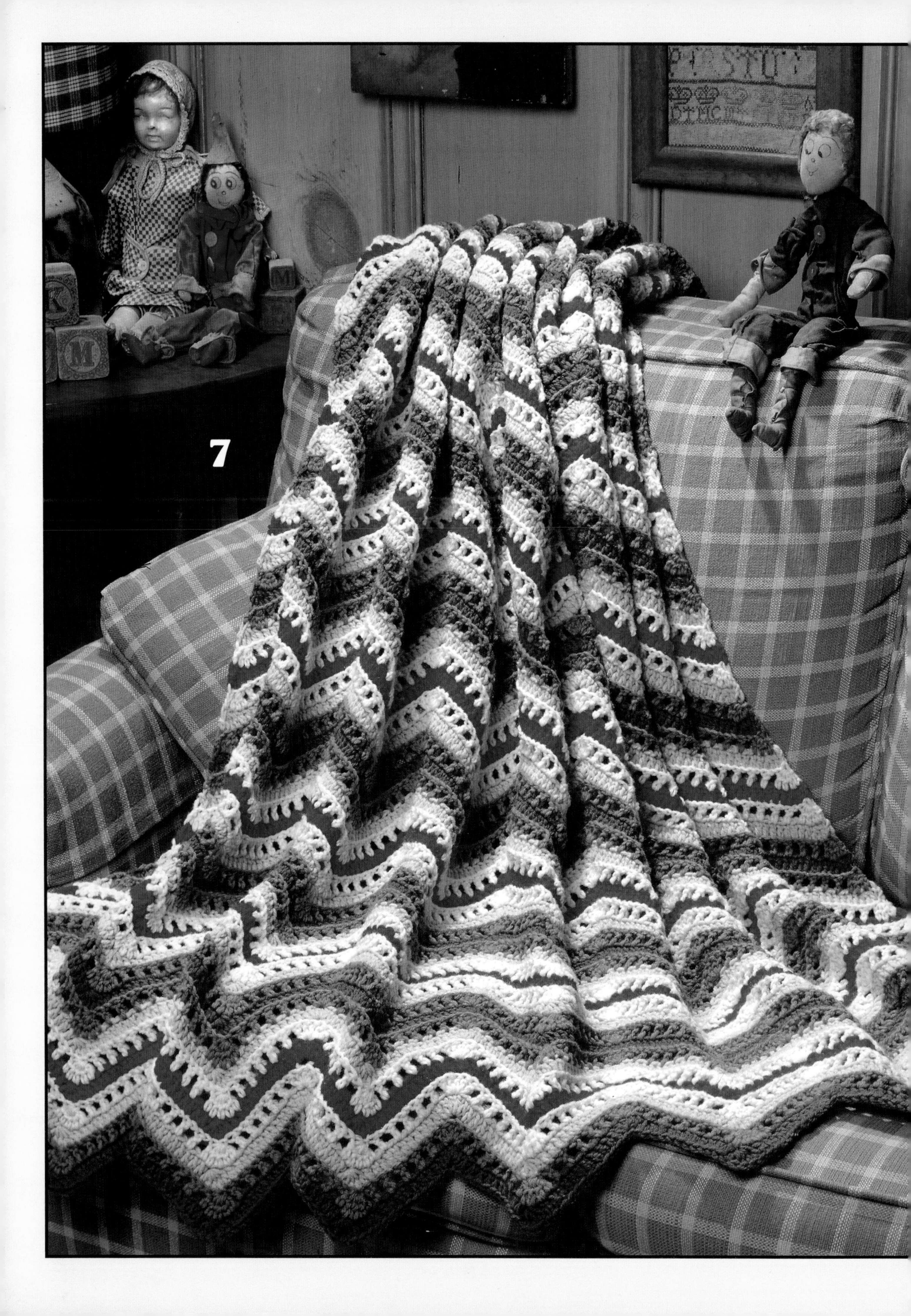
7

9

11. RUSTIC RIPPLE

Finished Size: Approximately 48" x 60"

MATERIALS

Worsted Weight Yarn, approximately:
- Color A (Green) - 19 ounces, (540 grams, 1,195 yards)
- Color B (Grey) - 38 ounces, (1,080 grams, 2,390 yards)
- Color C (Natural) - 18 ounces, (510 grams, 1,130 yards)

Crochet hook, size I (5.50 mm) **or** size needed for gauge

GAUGE: One repeat from point to point and 10 rows = 4"

Gauge Swatch: (8" x 4")
Ch 37 **loosely**.
Work same as Afghan for 10 rows.
Finish off.

COLOR SEQUENCE
4 Rows **each**: Color A, ★ Color B, Color C, Color B, Color A; repeat from ★ throughout ***(Fig. 3, page 1)***.

With Color A, ch 217 **loosely**.

Row 1: Dc in fourth ch from hook and in next 7 chs, ch 3, dc in next 8 chs, ★ skip next 2 chs, dc in next 8 chs, ch 3, dc in next 8 chs; repeat from ★ across: 193 sts and 12 ch-3 sps.

To work **Front Post double crochet *(abbreviated FPdc)***, YO, insert hook from **front** to **back** around post of st indicated ***(Fig. 4, page 1)***, YO and pull up a loop, (YO and draw through 2 loops on hook) twice. Skip st behind FPdc.

Row 2 (Right side)**:** Ch 2, turn; work FPdc around each of next 7 dc, (dc, ch 1, dc) in next ch-3 sp, ★ work FPdc around each of next 7 dc, skip next 2 dc, work FPdc around each of next 7 dc, (dc, ch 1, dc) in next ch-3 sp; repeat from ★ 10 times **more**, work FPdc around each of next 6 dc, skip next dc, work FPdc around next dc, leave last st unworked: 193 sts and 12 ch-1 sps.

Row 3: Ch 2, turn; work FPdc around each of next 7 sts, (dc, ch 1, dc) in next ch-1 sp, ★ work FPdc around each of next 7 sts, skip next 2 FPdc, work FPdc around each of next 7 sts, (dc, ch 1, dc) in next ch-1 sp; repeat from ★ 10 times **more**, work FPdc around each of next 6 sts, skip next FPdc, work FPdc around next FPdc, leave last st unworked.

Repeat Row 3 until Afghan measures approximately 60" from beginning ch, ending by working 4 rows Color A.

Finish off.

12. INDIAN SUMMER RIPPLE

Finished Size: Approximately 49" x 62"

MATERIALS

Worsted Weight Yarn, approximately:
- Color A (Black) - 14 ounces, (400 grams, 880 yards)
- Color B (Rust) - 10 ounces, (280 grams, 630 yards)
- Color C (Ecru) - 18 ounces, (510 grams, 1,130 yards)
- Color D (Teal) - 9 ounces, (260 grams, 565 yards)

Crochet hook, size H (5.00 mm) **or** size needed for gauge

GAUGE: 3 Repeats from point to point = $5^1/_4$" and 8 rows = 3"

Gauge Swatch: (7" x 3")
Ch 39 **loosely**.
Work same as Afghan for 8 rows.
Finish off.

COLOR SEQUENCE
One row Color A, 3 rows Color B, one row Color A, ★ 3 rows Color C, one row Color A, 3 rows Color D, one row Color A, 3 rows Color C, one row Color A, 3 rows Color B, one row Color A; repeat from ★ throughout ***(Fig. 3, page 1)***.

With Color A, ch 255 **loosely**.

Row 1 (Right side)**:** Sc in second ch from hook and in next 4 chs, 3 sc in next ch, ★ sc in next 3 chs, skip next 2 chs, sc in next 3 chs, 3 sc in next ch; repeat from ★ across to last 5 chs, sc in last 5 chs: 256 sc.

To **decrease**, pull up a loop in next 2 sc, YO and draw through all 3 loops on hook **(counts as one sc)**.

Row 2: Ch 1, turn; working in Back Loops Only ***(Fig. 1, page 1)***, decrease, sc in next 4 sc, 3 sc in next sc, ★ sc in next 3 sc, skip next 2 sc, sc in next 3 sc, 3 sc in next sc; repeat from ★ across to last 6 sc, sc in next 4 sc, decrease: 256 sc.

Repeat Row 2 until Afghan measures approximately 62" from beginning ch, ending by working one row Color A.

Finish off.

13. OCEAN WAVES RIPPLE

Finished Size: Approximately 48" x 60"

MATERIALS
Worsted Weight Yarn, approximately:
Color A (Dark Blue) - 8 ounces, (230 grams, 595 yards)
Color B (Medium Blue) - 7 ounces, (200 grams, 520 yards)
Color C (Blue) - 7 ounces, (200 grams, 520 yards)
Color D (Light Blue) - 7 ounces, (200 grams, 520 yards)
Crochet hook, size I (5.50 mm) **or** size needed for gauge

GAUGE: One repeat from point to point = 4¾"
and 8 rows = 5¼"

Gauge Swatch: (9½" x 5¼")
Ch 42 **loosely**.
Work same as Afghan for 8 rows.
Finish off.

PATTERN STITCHES
TREBLE CROCHET ***(abbreviated tr)***
YO twice, insert hook in st indicated, YO and pull up a loop, (YO and draw through 2 loops on hook) 3 times.

CLUSTER (uses next 3 sts)
YO twice, insert hook in **next** st, YO and pull up a loop, (YO and draw through 2 loops on hook) twice, YO twice, skip **next** st, insert hook in **next** st, YO and pull up a loop, (YO and draw through 2 loops on hook) twice, YO and draw through all 3 loops on hook.

COLOR SEQUENCE
2 Rows **each**: Color A, ★ Color B, Color C, Color D, Color A; repeat from ★ throughout ***(Fig. 3, page 1)***.

With Color A, ch 194 **loosely**.

Row 1 (Right side)**:** Tr in fifth ch from hook **(4 skipped chs count as first tr)**, (ch 1, tr in same st) twice, skip next ch, (tr in next ch, skip next ch) 3 times, work Cluster, skip next ch, (tr in next ch, skip next ch) 3 times, **[**(tr, ch 1) twice, 2 tr)**]** in next ch, ★ **[**2 tr, (ch 1, tr) twice**]** in next ch, skip next ch, (tr in next ch, skip next ch) 3 times, work Cluster, skip next ch, (tr in next ch, skip next ch) 3 times, **[**(tr, ch 1) twice, 2 tr**]** in next ch; repeat from ★ across: 150 sts and 40 ch-1 sps.

Row 2: Ch 1, turn; sc in each st and in each ch-1 sp across: 190 sc.

Row 3: Ch 4 **(counts as first tr)**, turn; tr in same st, (ch 1, tr in same st) twice, skip next sc, (tr in next sc, skip next sc) 3 times, work Cluster, skip next sc, (tr in next sc, skip next sc) 3 times, **[**(tr, ch 1) twice, 2 tr**]** in next sc, ★ **[**2 tr, (ch 1, tr) twice**]** in next sc, skip next sc, (tr in next sc, skip next sc) 3 times, work Cluster, skip next sc, (tr in next sc, skip next sc) 3 times, **[**(tr, ch 1) twice, 2 tr**]** in next sc; repeat from ★ across.

Row 4: Ch 1, turn; sc in each st and in each ch-1 sp across.

Repeat Rows 3 and 4 until Afghan measures approximately 60" from beginning ch, ending by working 2 rows Color A.

Finish off.

6

5

14. ROLLING HILLS RIPPLE

Finished Size: Approximately 48" x 64"

MATERIALS

Worsted Weight Yarn, approximately:
- Color A (Light Green) - 18 ounces, (510 grams, 1,185 yards)
- Color B (Green) - 14 ounces, (400 grams, 920 yards)
- Color C (Dark Green) - 7 ounces, (200 grams, 460 yards)
- Color D (Ecru) - 4 ounces, (110 grams, 265 yards)

Crochet hook, size H (5.00 mm) **or** size needed for gauge

GAUGE: One repeat from point to point = 7¼"
and 7 rows = 5½"

Gauge Swatch: (12" x 5½")
Ch 63 **loosely**.
Work same as Afghan for 7 rows.
Finish off.

PATTERN STITCHES

3-DC CLUSTER (uses next 3 sts)
★ YO, insert hook in **next** st, YO and pull up a loop, YO and draw through 2 loops on hook; repeat from ★ 2 times **more**, YO and draw through all 4 loops on hook.

5-DC CLUSTER (uses next 5 sts)
★ YO, insert hook in **next** st, YO and pull up a loop, YO and draw through 2 loops on hook; repeat from ★ 4 times **more**, YO and draw through all 6 loops on hook.

SHELL
Dc in st indicated, (ch 1, dc in same st) twice.

COLOR SEQUENCE
4 Rows Color A, ★ 2 rows Color B, one row **each**: Color C, Color D, Color C, 2 rows Color B, 4 rows Color A; repeat from ★ throughout ***(Fig. 3, page 1)***.

With Color A, ch 243 **loosely**.

Row 1 (Right side)**:** YO, insert hook in fourth ch from hook **(3 skipped chs count as first dc)**, YO and pull up a loop, YO and draw through 2 loops on hook, (YO, insert hook in **next** ch, YO and pull up a loop, YO and draw through 2 loops on hook) twice, YO and draw through all 4 loops on hook, dc in next 8 chs, work Shell in next ch, dc in next 8 chs, ★ work 5-dc Cluster, dc in next 4 chs, work Shell in next ch, dc in next 4 chs, work 5-dc Cluster, dc in next 8 chs, work Shell in next ch, dc in next 8 chs; repeat from ★ across to last 4 chs, work 3-dc Cluster, dc in last ch: 215 sts and 26 ch-1 sps.

Row 2: Ch 3 **(counts as first dc)**, turn; working in Back Loops Only ***(Fig. 1, page 1)***, work 3-dc Cluster, dc in next 7 dc and in next ch, work Shell in next dc, dc in next ch and in next 7 dc, ★ work 5 dc-Cluster, dc in next 3 dc and in next ch, work Shell in next dc, dc in next ch and in next 3 dc, work 5-dc Cluster, dc in next 7 dc and in next ch, work Shell in next dc, dc in next ch and in next 7 dc; repeat from ★ across to last 4 sts, work 3-dc Cluster, dc in last dc.

Repeat Row 2 until Afghan measures approximately 64" from beginning ch, ending by working 4 rows Color A.

Finish off.

15. SPRING BLOSSOM RIPPLE

Finished Size: Approximately 49" x 61"

MATERIALS

Worsted Weight Yarn, approximately:
- Color A (Dark Green) - 13 ounces, (370 grams, 855 yards)
- Color B (White) - 13 ounces, (370 grams, 855 yards)
- Color C (Green) - 10 ounces, (280 grams, 655 yards)
- Color D (Pink) - 5 ounces, (140 grams, 330 yards)

Crochet hook, size H (5.00 mm) **or** size needed for gauge

GAUGE: One repeat from point to point = $3^1/_4$"
and 7 rows = 5"

Gauge Swatch: (7" x 5")
Ch 35 **loosely**.
Work same as Afghan for 7 rows.
Finish off.

PATTERN STITCHES

CLUSTER (uses next 5 sts)
YO, insert hook in **next** st, YO and pull up a loop, YO and draw through 2 loops on hook, YO, skip **next** 3 sts, insert hook in **next** st, YO and pull up a loop, YO and draw through 2 loops on hook, YO and draw through all 3 loops on hook.

DECREASE (uses next 3 sts)
YO, insert hook in **next** dc, YO and pull up a loop, YO and draw through 2 loops on hook, YO, skip **next** st, insert hook in **next** dc, YO and pull up a loop, YO and draw through 2 loops on hook, YO and draw through all 3 loops on hook.

COLOR SEQUENCE

One row Color A, 3 rows Color B, one row **each**: Color A, ★ Color C, Color D, Color C, Color A, 3 rows Color B, one row Color A; repeat from ★ throughout ***(Fig. 3, page 1)***.

With Color A, ch 230 **loosely**.

Row 1 (Right side)**:** Dc in fifth ch from hook and in next 5 chs **(4 skipped chs count as first dc plus one skipped ch)**, 2 dc in next ch, ch 3, 2 dc in next ch, ★ dc in next 4 chs, work Cluster, dc in next 4 chs, 2 dc in next ch, ch 3, 2 dc in next ch; repeat from ★ across to last 8 chs, dc in next 6 chs, skip next ch, dc in last ch: 200 sts and 15 ch-3 sps.

Note: Loop a short piece of yarn around any stitch to mark last row as **right** side.

Row 2: Ch 3 **(counts as first dc, now and throughout)**, turn; working in both loops, skip next 2 dc, dc in next dc, ch 1, skip next dc, (dc in next dc, ch 1, skip next dc) twice, (dc, ch 3, dc) in next ch-3 sp, ★ ch 1, skip next dc, (dc in next dc, ch 1, skip next dc) twice, decrease, ch 1, skip next dc, (dc in next dc, ch 1, skip next dc) twice, (dc, ch 3, dc) in next ch-3 sp; repeat from ★ across to last 9 dc, (ch 1, skip next dc, dc in next dc) 3 times, skip next 2 dc, dc in last dc: 108 sts and 105 sps.

Row 3: Ch 3, turn; skip next dc, (dc in next ch-1 sp and in next dc) 3 times, (2 dc, ch 3, 2 dc) in next ch-3 sp, ★ (dc in next dc and in next ch-1 sp) twice, work Cluster, (dc in next ch-1 sp and in next dc) twice, (2 dc, ch 3, 2 dc) in next ch-3 sp; repeat from ★ across to last 8 sts, (dc in next dc and in next ch-1 sp) 3 times, skip next dc, dc in last dc: 200 sts and 15 ch-3 sps.

Rows 4 and 5: Repeat Rows 2 and 3.

Rows 6-9: Ch 3, turn; working in Back Loops Only ***(Fig. 1, page 1)***, skip next 2 dc, dc in next 6 dc, (2 dc, ch 3, 2 dc) in next ch-3 sp, ★ dc in next 4 dc, work Cluster, dc in next 4 dc, (2 dc, ch 3, 2 dc) in next ch-3 sp; repeat from ★ across to last 9 dc, dc in next 6 dc, skip next 2 dc, dc in last dc.

Repeat Rows 2-9 until Afghan measures approximately 61" from beginning ch, ending by working Row 5 and one row Color A.

Finish off.

With Color A, add 9 strands of fringe at each point across short edges of Afghan ***(Figs. 5a & b, page 1)***.

Great Dinner Parties
BARBARA MY
COOKING IN YOUR MICROWAVE
1

10

16. RAINBOW RIPPLE

Finished Size: Approximately 47" x 60"

MATERIALS

Worsted Weight Yarn, approximately:
- Color A (Pink) - 6 ounces, (170 grams, 395 yards)
- Color B (White) - 6 ounces, (170 grams, 395 yards)
- Color C (Peach) - 5 ounces, (140 grams, 330 yards)
- Color D (Yellow) - 5 ounces, (140 grams, 330 yards)
- Color E (Green) - 5 ounces, (140 grams, 330 yards)
- Color F (Blue) - 5 ounces, (140 grams, 330 yards)
- Color G (Lavender) - 5 ounces, (140 grams, 330 yards)

Crochet hook, size I (5.50 mm) **or** size needed for gauge

GAUGE: One repeat from point to point = 5¼"
and 7 rows = 4½"

Gauge Swatch: (10½" x 4½")
Ch 51 **loosely**.
Work same as Afghan for 7 rows.
Finish off.

PATTERN STITCHES

DECREASE (uses next 2 sts or sps)
★ YO, insert hook in **next** st or sp, YO and pull up a loop, YO and draw through 2 loops on hook; repeat from ★ once **more**, YO and draw through all 3 loops on hook **(counts as one dc)**.

V-STITCH ***(abbreviated V-St)***
(Dc, ch 1, dc) in next st.

COLOR SEQUENCE

3 Rows Color A, one row Color B, ★ 3 rows Color C, one row Color B, 3 rows Color D, one row Color B, 3 rows Color E, one row Color B, 3 rows Color F, one row Color B, 3 rows Color G, one row Color B, 3 rows Color A, one row Color B; repeat from ★ 3 times **more** ***(Fig. 3, page 1)***.

With Color A, ch 219 **loosely**.

Row 1 (Right side)**:** 2 Dc in fourth ch from hook **(3 skipped chs count as first dc)**, dc in next 8 chs, decrease, skip next 2 chs, decrease, dc in next 8 chs, ★ work V-St twice, dc in next 8 chs, decrease, skip next 2 chs, decrease, dc in next 8 chs; repeat from ★ across to last ch, 3 dc in last ch: 200 dc and 16 ch-1 sps.

Note: Loop a short piece of yarn around any stitch to mark last row as **right** side.

Rows 2 and 3: Ch 3 **(counts as first dc, now and throughout)**, turn; 2 dc in same st, dc in next 8 dc, decrease, skip next 2 dc, decrease, ★ dc in next 7 dc and in next ch-1 sp, work V-St twice, dc in next ch-1 sp and in next 7 dc, decrease, skip next 2 dc, decrease; repeat from ★ across to last 9 dc, dc in next 8 dc, 3 dc in last dc.

Row 4: Ch 1, turn; sc in first dc, ch 1, (skip next dc, sc in next dc, ch 1) 4 times, skip next dc, sc in next 4 dc, ch 1, (skip next dc, sc in next dc, ch 1) 4 times, ★ skip next ch, sc in next 2 dc, ch 1, (skip next st, sc in next dc, ch 1) 4 times, skip next dc, sc in next 4 dc, ch 1, (skip next dc, sc in next dc, ch 1) 4 times; repeat from ★ across to last 2 dc, skip next dc, sc in last dc: 126 sc and 90 ch-1 sps.

Row 5: Ch 3, turn; 2 dc in same st, (dc in next ch-1 sp and in next sc) 4 times, decrease, skip next 2 sc, decrease, (dc in next sc and in next ch-1 sp) 4 times, ★ work V-St twice, (dc in next ch-1 sp and in next sc) 4 times, decrease, skip next 2 sc, decrease, (dc in next sc and in next ch-1 sp) 4 times; repeat from ★ across to last sc, 3 dc in last sc: 200 dc and 16 ch-1 sps.

Rows 6 and 7: Ch 3, turn; 2 dc in same st, dc in next 8 dc, decrease, skip next 2 dc, decrease, ★ dc in next 7 dc and in next ch-1 sp, work V-St twice, dc in next ch-1 sp and in next 7 dc, decrease, skip next 2 dc, decrease; repeat from ★ across to last 9 dc, dc in next 8 dc, 3 dc in last dc.

Rows 8-100: Repeat Rows 4-7, 23 times; then repeat Row 4 once **more**.

Finish off.

BOTTOM EDGING

Row 1: With **wrong** side facing and working in free loops of beginning ch ***(Fig. 2, page 1)***, join Color B with slip st in first ch (at base of first 3 dc); ch 1, sc in same st, ch 1, (skip next ch, sc in next ch, ch 1) 4 times, skip next ch, sc in next 2 chs, ch 1, sc in next 2 chs, ch 1, (skip next ch, sc in next ch, ch 1) 3 times, ★ skip next ch, sc in next 2 chs, skip next 2 chs, sc in next 2 chs, ch 1, (skip next ch, sc in next ch, ch 1) 3 times, skip next ch, sc in next 2 chs, ch 1, sc in next 2 chs, ch 1, (skip next ch, sc in next ch, ch 1) 3 times; repeat from ★ across to last 4 chs, skip next ch, sc in next ch, ch 1, skip next ch, sc in last ch; finish off.

Afghans made and instructions tested by Connie Balogh, JoAnn Bowling, Delois Bynum, Linda Graves, Carolyn Lee, Faye Morgan, Angie New, Janelle Oliger, Dale Potter, Rondi Rowell, Donna Soellner, Faith Stewart, Karan Stewart, and Bill Tanner.